Gourmet Freshwater FISH RECIPES

Quick & Easy Recipes
by Dr. Duane R. Lund

Author of
101 Favorite Freshwater Fish Recipes

Distributed by
ADVENTURE PUBLICATIONS
820 Cleveland Street South
Cambridge, Minnesota 55008

ISBN-13: 978-0934860-09-3
ISBN-10: 0-934860-09-2

Gourmet Freshwater Fish Recipes

First Printing, 1993
Second Printing, 1994
Third Printing, 1997
Fourth Printing, 2001
Fifth Printing, 2006
Sixth Printing, 2011

Printed in the United States of America
by
Lund S&R Publications
Staples, Minnesota 56479

DEDICATION
To all those who have patiently put
up with all my experimenting

TABLE OF CONTENTS

CHAPTER III
WALLEYES

CHAPTER IV
NORTHERN PIKE

CHAPTER V
MUSKIES

CHAPTER VI
SALMON

CHAPTER VII
LAKE TROUT

CHAPTER VIII
STREAM TROUT

CHAPTER IX
PERCH

CHAPTER X
CATFISH AND BULLHEADS

CHAPTER XI
EELPOUT

CHAPTER XII
WHITEFISH

CHAPTER XIII
SMELT

CHAPTER XIV
FISH STOCKS, TARTAR SAUCES, HERBS AND SPICES

INTRODUCTION

"101 Favorite Freshwater Fish Recipes" was published in 1979. In the ensuing years it has been reprinted seven times. Every so often we receive letters asking if there will be a sequel, so along about 1990-we began collecting and creating another hundred or so new, quality recipes for freshwater fish. This time the recipes have been categorized by species of fish — but that does not mean that a bass recipe, for example, will work only for bass. Be assured that most any of the recipes for white-meated fish will work for all such varieties. Likewise, a recipe for a red-meated fish, such as salmon, will probably work well for lake trout. Cross-over may also be tried with the assurance that the product will be palatable.

In most cases these recipes will also work with ocean fish.

It is so easy to get stuck in a comfortable rut of just fixing fish one or two ways. Such cooks and their guests are missing a great deal of dining pleasure. Besides, it is possible to get tired of fish prepared the same way time after time. We can truly enjoy it more by cooking it differently.

The recipes which follow may also give you ideas for recipes of your own. You are encouraged to experiment.

So read on — and then ENJOY!

CHAPTER I

PANFISH

Giant panfish: a 3 pound crappie and two 1 pound plus sunfish from Leech Lake (Minnesota).

By "panfish" we mean the several varieties of crappies and sunfish found in North America. The recipes which follow work equally well for all. Keep in mind that as stated in the Introduction most of the recipes found in this book may be used on other varieties of freshwater fish. It is particularly proper to use recipes for white-meated fish with other varieties of white-meated fish, likewise recipes for red-meated fish, such as salmon will work well for trout. Please don't think of any of the recipes found in this book as being limited to the specific species where it appears. They will even work with ocean fish. On the other hand, we guarantee satisfaction only with the particular variety where it is given! But you are encouraged to experiment. Be brave!

Whole Panfish Stuffed with Crabmeat

8 whole crappies (about $\frac{3}{4}$ pound live weight) or 12 whole sunfish (about $\frac{1}{2}$ pound live weight). Adjust numbers to the size of the fish. Serves four.

> 1 egg
> $\frac{3}{4}$ cup hot water
> $\frac{1}{2}$ pound crabmeat
> 1 cup bread crumbs
> $\frac{1}{3}$ cup chopped onion (fine)
> 1 t parsley flakes (or 1 T fresh parsley, chopped)
> $\frac{1}{2}$ t oregano
> 1 T lemon juice
> $\frac{1}{4}$ pound butter, melted
> $\frac{1}{4}$ t Worcestershire sauce
> salt and pepper to taste
> paprika (a dusting for each fish)

Scale and remove head, fins and entrails. Wash clean and pat dry with paper towel. Sprinkle lightly, inside and out, with salt and pepper.

Sauté the chopped onion in butter (or oil) until translucent; add crabmeat and continue to sauté for another 3 minutes.

Place the bread crumbs in a bowl. Add water, egg, $\frac{1}{8}$ pound melted butter, the parsley, Worcestershire sauce, oregano, lemon juice, onion, crabmeat and a little salt and pepper (depending on your taste). Stir together until evenly mixed.

Stuff each of the fish and lay them on a greased (or sprayed with vegetable oil) baking sheet or open baking dish. Brush the fish with the remainder of the butter and sprinkle lightly with the paprika.

Bake in a pre-heated 400° oven for about 20 minutes or until the skin is crisp and golden brown. The fish should flake with a fork and be opaque looking.

Serve whole.

Deep-fried Panfish Fillets with Sprite Batter

$8\frac{3}{4}$ pound crappies (live weight) or 12 half-pound sunfish.

If fish are a different size, adjust numbers accordingly. Four servings.

> 1 cup "complete" pancake flour
> 1 can Sprite soda (or carbonated water or
> other lemon-lime beverage)

You will not need the whole can.

Fillet and skin the panfish. Wash clean and pat dry with paper towel. Season on one side lightly with salt and pepper.

Prepare batter by adding the carbonated beverage — a little at a time — to the pancake flour, stirring together until a light batter is formed. (A little thinner than you would use for pancakes).

Meanwhile, heat oil in the French fryer.

Dip the fillets in the batter and then place them — two or three at a time — in the hot oil. (Too many fillets at one time will cool the oil and make the fillets greasy.) When a light brown, remove the fillets and place them on paper towel to drain.

Serve with a tartar sauce.

Whole Panfish with Tomato Sauce and Garlic

8 whole crappies about ¾ pound each or 12 whole sunfish, about ½ pound each live weight. Adjust the number of fish to the size of the fish. Four servings.

> 4 cloves garlic, chopped very fine
> 1 T tomato paste
> 4 drops Tabasco sauce
> 1 T lemon juice
> water
> salt and pepper to taste
> 1 T bread or cracker crumbs
> ½ cup cooking oil

Scale fish; remove heads, fins and entrails. Wash clean and dry with paper towel.

Season fish lightly, inside and out, with salt and pepper.

Stir together the oil, lemon juice, tomato paste, Tabasco sauce, garlic and 1 cup of water — in a skillet. Cook gently over low-medium heat until it begins to boil. Add the fish, cover, and cook five minutes. Turn the fish and continue to cook until the fish is done (can be flaked with a fork). Unless you have a large skillet, you probably will not be able to cook all the fish at once. It doesn't matter. Using the same liquid, cook the rest of the fish. Keep all of the cooked fish warm (in the oven).

When all of the fish have been cooked, add the crumbs and ½ cup of water to the sauce in the pan. Continue to cook and stir until it thickens some (about 5 minutes). Lay the fish side by side and spoon some of the sauce over each.

Fillets with Mushroom Sauce

8 crappies about ¾ pound each live weight or 12 sunfish about ½ pound each live weight. Adjust the numbers of fish to compensate for differences in weight if the fish are larger or smaller. Serves 4.

> 1 cup of flour
> salt and pepper to taste
> 1 cup mushrooms, chopped, but in fairly large pieces
> 2 T chopped onion
> ½ t garlic, finely chopped
> ¼ cup white wine
> ⅛ pound butter, cut into small pats

cooking oil or butter or margarine for frying fish
Fillet the fish, wash and clean, dry on paper towel.
Lightly season with salt and pepper.
Dredge fillets in flour and sauté over medium heat until brown on both sides. Keep the fillets warm in the oven.

Using the same pan, add all other ingredients, continue to cook, stirring in the butter one pat at a time until all are melted. Display fillets on a platter and spoon sauce on the center of each.

Pickled Panfish with Dill

Here is an opportunity to use those small sunnies or crappies.

4 pounds of panfish, weighed after scaling and removing heads, fins and entrails. Cut into 1½ inch chunks (herring size); you may leave the smaller fish whole.

> 1 cup pickling salt
> 1½ cups sugar
> 1 cup pickling salt
> white vinegar — enough to cover the fish
> 3 large onions, sliced thin and broken into circles
> 4 T pickling spices
> 4 sprigs (top 6 inches) of dill
> 2 bay leaves

Place the fish chunks in a glass or stone jar. Cover with cold water. Stir in the pickling salt and refrigerate — at least 24 hours.

After 24 hours, remove the fish, wash thoroughly, and drain on paper towel. Place the fish in a stone or glass container. Add all remaining ingredients and the fish and add enough vinegar to cover the fish chunks. Gently stir until the sugar has dissolved.

Refrigerate 48 hours before serving. Continue to keep refrigerated.

Whole Panfish baked in cream —a Scandinavian specialty

8 crappies (about ¾ pound each) or 12 sunfish (about ½ pound each).

Scale and remove heads, fins and entrails. Wash and pat dry.

> 1 cup cream (half and half works well)
> 1 green pepper, cut into rings
> 3 T chopped chives
> 2 T parsley, chopped
> salt and pepper to taste

Season the fish, inside and out, with salt and pepper. Place in a shallow baking dish. Lay pepper rings on the fish. Sprinkle fish with chives and parsley. Pour the cream in so that it doesn't quite cover the fish. Bake in a preheated 350° oven 30 minutes or until the fish flakes with a fork. Serve on a platter. Spoon the cream over each fish. If the chives and parsley have floated off the fish, rescue them with a slotted spoon and sprinkle over the cooked fish.

Fillets with Salsa and Dill — Microwave

8 three quarter pound crappies (live weight) or 12 half pound sunfish (live weight). If fish average larger or smaller, adjust the numbers. Serves 4.

> 1½ cups mild salsa sauce
> 2 T dill, chopped fine (or 1 t dillweed)
> 2 T lemon juice

Fillet the panfish, wash and pat dry with paper towel.

Arrange the fillets on a microwave-compatible plate. If the tail ends of the fillets are much thinner than the rest of the fillets. fold under so as to have as even a thickness as possible. Sprinkle with lemon juice. Cover with paper towel. Microwave on high for about 3 minutes until the fish are opaque and/or flake with a fork.

Meanwhile, stir the chopped dill into the salsa. Heat and serve over the cooked fish.

Cheri's Baked Sunfish Fillets *

> 1 to 2 dozen sunfish fillets (crappies also work well)
> ½ cup cornmeal
> 1 cup flour
> 2 eggs (scrambled into ¼ cup milk)
> 3 T butter
> 2½ cups instant potatoes (flakes)
> salt and pepper to taste

Combine the flour and cornmeal.

In a separate bowl mix the eggs into the milk.

Place the potato flakes in a separate bowl.

Salt and pepper the fillets.

Dip the fish first into the flour-cornmeal mixture, then into the egg-milk mixture and last into the potato flakes.

Meanwhile, melt the butter in a baking dish or large cake pan at 400° for 2 minutes or until it is melted.

Bake the fish for 10 to 15 minutes or until brown on the bottom side; turn and bake another 10 to 15 minutes until brown on both sides so that they will be a golden brown and crispy. Enjoy!

* courtesy Cheri Brager, Deerwood, MN

CHAPTER II

BASS

A string of smallmouths from the Lake of the Woods.

The recipes in this chapter are appropriate for either large or smallmouth bass — even though the flavors are somewhat different.

If the fish come from muddy or quite weedy water, it may be wise to not use the stomach meat — which could contain a stronger or more "fishy" taste. Bass is one of the more flavorful fish and the taste can truly be enhanced with sauces and seasonings.

Marinated and Fried Bass Fillets

2 pounds skinned fillets cut into serving size pieces. Serves 4.

Marinade Ingredients
½ cup milk
1 egg white — beaten lightly
2 T soy sauce
1 t garlic powder
1 T chopped dill

Frying Ingredients
cooking oil, butter or margarine
1 cup bread or cracker crumbs
2 T Parmesan cheese (grated)

Stir together the marinade ingredients. Place fillets in a single layer in a flat dish. Pour the marinade over the fish. Refrigerate 15 minutes. Turn the fillets — thus coating both sides. Refrigerate another 15 minutes. Discard the marinade.

Thoroughly mix together the crumbs and the cheese. Coat both sides of each fillet and fry in light oil until brown on both sides. (If you have difficulty getting the crumbs and cheese to stick to the fillets, mix 1 egg in a cup of water and dip the fillets in the egg wash first.)

Spicy Broiled Fillets of Bass

> 2 pounds bass fillets, skinned and cut into serving size pieces. Serves 4.
>
> 2 cloves garlic, minced but not too fine
>
> 2 T cracked pepper (coarse ground)

Sauce Ingredients

> 4 T olive oil
>
> 2 T white vinegar
>
> 2 T Parmesan cheese (grated)
>
> 2 cloves garlic, minced very fine
>
> 3 drops Tabasco sauce

Literally press the coarse pepper and garlic into the fillets — both sides. Broil on a hot grill that has been sprayed or brushed with vegetable oil.

Broil 5 or 6 minutes or until the fish flakes with a fork. Do not over-cook.

Meanwhile, prepare the sauce by placing the 5 ingredients in a blender for 15 to 20 seconds. Sprinkle lightly over each broiled fillet.

Whole Bass Baked in Milk

> 1 - 3 to 4 pound bass (live weight), scaled and dressed. Serves 4.
>
> 1 cup celery, chopped
>
> 1 large onion, chopped
>
> ¼ cup fresh parsley, chopped
>
> salt and pepper to taste
>
> 1 T lemon juice
>
> 3 T butter or margarine
>
> Milk

Scale the bass. Remove head, fins and entrails. Wash clean and pat dry inside and out. Rub the inside of the fish with lemon juice and lightly salt and pepper the fish inside and out.

Sauté the chopped onion and celery in butter or margarine until the onion is translucent.

Combine the onion, celery and parsley and stuff the cavity;

set the fish on its stomach in a baking dish or roasting pan. (If you have trouble with the stuffing falling out, use foil to hold it in.)

Add enough milk to nearly cover the fish (about ¾ of the fish).

Bake in a pre-heated 325° oven for an hour or until the fish flakes with a fork in the large end. Discard the stuffing. Cut fish into serving-size cross sections.

Bass Fillets Baked in Cornbread

2 pounds bass fillets — skinned, washed and dried. Four servings.

2 cups cornmeal

1 t salt

1 T baking soda

2 eggs

1½ cups milk

2 T cooking oil

pepper to taste

Mix together the cornmeal, salt and baking soda. In another bowl, stir together the eggs, milk and cooking oil. Now combine and stir together all ingredients.

Cut fillets into serving size pieces.

Spread a layer of the batter in a cake pan. Lay the fillets on top (single layer). Sprinkle lightly with pepper. Cover with the remaining batter.

Bake in a pre-heated hot oven (400°) for about 20 minutes or until a toothpick inserted in the cornbread comes out clean.

Spread softened butter or margarine over the cornbread and enjoy it with the fish.

Baked Bass Fillets with Creole Sauce

> 2 pounds bass fillets — skinned, washed and dried. Four servings.
>
> 3 T parsley flakes or 4 T chopped fresh parsley.
>
> *Creole Sauce Ingredients*
> 1 cup tomatoes, diced
> $\frac{1}{2}$ cup celery, chopped fairly fine
> 1 small onion, chopped fairly fine
> 4 T green pepper, chopped - not as fine
> 2 T tomato paste
> $\frac{1}{2}$ t oregano
> $\frac{1}{2}$ t basil
> $\frac{3}{4}$ cup chicken broth (may use broth from canned chicken soup)
> $\frac{1}{2}$ t Tobasco sauce

To prepare the sauce, sauté the onions and celery in oil or butter until the former are translucent. Add all other ingredients, stir together and cook over low heat (barely bubbling) for 5 minutes.

Cut fillets into serving size pieces.

Arrange the fillets in a single layer in a baking dish which has been coated with cooking oil or spray. Spoon the sauce over the fillets and bake in a pre-heated 350° oven for about 20 minutes or until the fish can be flaked with a fork.

Move the fillets to a serving dish. Spoon the sauce over the fish.

Sprinkle with parsley.

Baked Bass Fillets with Rhubarb-Breadcrumb Coating

> 2 pounds skinned bass fillets, washed and dried. Serves 4.
>
> $\frac{1}{2}$ cup rhubarb, chopped fine and sweetened with 1 T sugar
> $1\frac{1}{2}$ cups bread crumbs
> $\frac{1}{4}$ pound butter, melted
> salt and pepper to taste

Combine the rhubarb, crumbs, melted butter, salt and pepper and gently stir together. Arrange the fillets on a lightly greased baking sheet. Sprinkle the rhubarb-crumb mixture over each fillet, forming a thin layer or coating.

Bake in a pre-heated 400° oven for about 15 minutes or until the crust is a light brown and the fish is opaque or can be flaked with a fork.

Bass with Tomatoes and Wine

> 2 pounds bass fillets — skinned, washed and dried. Four servings.
>
> 1 cn. tomato sauce — Italian style
>
> 1 medium onion, sliced thin and broken into circles
>
> ½ cup stuffed olives, sliced
>
> ¼ cup black, pitted olives, sliced
>
> ½ cup white wine (or gin)
>
> salt and pepper to taste
>
> oil, butter or margarine to sauté onion

Sauté the onion circles until translucent. Add all other ingredients (except fish), gently stir together and let simmer for about 5 minutes.

Add fish pieces, (cut serving size) turning each to be sure both sides are well coated. Cook (covered) over medium heat about 10 minutes — turning the fish pieces about halfway through. Fish is done when it flakes with a fork.

Bass Fillets with Mayonnaise

> 2 pounds bass fillets, skinned, washed and dried. Serves four.
>
> 1 cup mayonnaise (lean)
>
> 3 T prepared mustard
>
> 1 t dill seed (or 1 T chopped dill — very fine)
>
> 1 T chopped parsley

Combine thoroughly the mayonnaise, mustard and dill.

Lay the fillets (serving size cuts) on a lightly greased baking sheet. Coat the topside of each piece with the mayonnaise mixture. Bake in a pre-heated 350° oven for 20 minutes or until

the fish flakes with a fork.
  Garnish with parsley.

Bass Fillets Baked in Cream
> 2 pounds fillets (skinned and cut into serving size pieces). Serves four.
> 1 large onion, sliced
> 3 T chopped celery
> 1½ cups cream
> 1 T chopped chives
> 1 T chopped dill
> 1 T chopped parsley
> salt and pepper

  Grease a baking dish. Lay the onion slices and celery on the bottom of the dish; next, a single layer of fillets. Lightly season with salt and pepper. Cover with cream. Sprinkle on herbs. Bake in pre-heated medium oven (about 45 minutes).

Baked Bass with Ham Stuffing
  Use about a four pound bass (live weight). Scale the fish, draw, and remove the head, tail, and fins. Rub fish inside and out with lemon juice or wedges. Season lightly — inside and out — with salt and pepper.
> Prepare stuffing from the following ingredients:
> 2 cups seasoned croutons
> 1 large onion, chopped (save 4 slices for baking)
> ¼ green pepper, chopped
> 1 cup celery, chopped
> ⅓ pound diced ham (Most any kind of ham luncheon meat will also work well)
> ¼ pound butter or margarine, melted
> ⅓ cup hot water
> 4 slices bacon

  Sauté the onion and celery in butter over low heat until onion is translucent.
  Add the chopped ham, green pepper, and hot water. Pour the mixture over the croutons and mix well.

Stuff the fish. *

Place a large sheet of foil (enough to wrap the entire fish) in the bottom of the roaster.

Make cross-section cuts on the back of the fish - about one inch deep and 1½ inches apart.

Place slices of onion and bacon, alternately, the length of the back of the fish (over each cut).

Pull the foil up around the fish and seal.

Place in an open roaster or baking dish and bake in a preheated 300° oven for about an hour and 15 minutes or until the fish flakes with a fork at the large end. Open the foil at the top and roll back halfway down the sides of the fish the last 15 minutes or so.

Cut into serving-size cross sections.

*Extra stuffing may be baked separately in foil.
Do not stuff the fish until just before you put it in the oven.

Zesty Bass Fillets

2 pounds bass fillets, skinned, washed and dried.
Four servings.
3 T chopped onion
2 garlic cloves, minced
1 t chopped tarragon
5 drops Tabasco sauce
salt and pepper (use sparingly)
¼ pound butter

Sauté the onion, garlic and tarragon until the onion is translucent. Stir in the 5 drops of Tabasco sauce.

Cut fillets into serving size pieces.

Salt and pepper the fillets on both sides (lightly) and add them to the skillet. Cook the fish over low-medium heat, turning after 5 minutes. Continue cooking another 5 minutes or until fish flakes with a fork.

Place the fillets on a platter and spoon sauce over the fish.

CHAPTER III
WALLEYES

Adam Clabots with a nice stringer of walleyes, Gull Lake, Brainerd, MN

Because of walleye's delicate but delicious flavor, the recipes which follow use seasonings sparingly.

Parmesan Walleye

> 2 pounds walleye fillets, skinned, washed and dried. Serves 4.
>
> 2 cups cracker crumbs (salted soda)
>
> ¾ cup grated Parmesan cheese
>
> 1 t oregano
>
> pepper to taste
>
> ¼ pound butter (or margarine), melted

Combine the crumbs, Parmesan and oregano; mix well. Sprinkle the fillets with pepper — both sides. No additional salt should be needed if you use salted crackers for the crumbs.

Dip the fillets in the butter and then in the crumb-cheese mix. Lay them side by side on a lightly greased baking sheet.

Bake in a pre-heated 350° oven for about 10 minutes on each side or until the fish flakes with a fork. Do not over-cook.

Walleye Baked in Foil

> 2 pounds walleye fillets, skinned, washed, and dried. Serves 4.
>
> 2 T olive oil (may substitute cooking oil, butter or margarine)
>
> 1 lemon, sliced
>
> 1 small onion, sliced and broken into rings
>
> 1 small green pepper, cut into rings
>
> 1 tomato, sliced
>
> salt and pepper to taste

Lubricate a sheet of foil — large enough so that it may be folded over to cover the fish. Lay the walleye fillets side by side and sprinkle lightly with salt and pepper. Scatter, alternately, lemon and tomato slices and rings of onion and green pepper. Fold over the foil and seal.

Bake in a pre-heated 350° oven or on a hot grill for about 15 minutes. Fish will flake with a fork when done. Don't over-cook; start checking for doneness after 10 minutes.

Almond Coated Walleye Fillets

> 2 pounds walleye fillets, skinned, washed and dried. Serves 4.
>
> 2 cups almonds (or cashews) crushed very fine
>
> salt and pepper to taste
>
> 1 egg
>
> 1 cup water
>
> cooking oil, butter or margarine

Cut the fillet into serving size pieces for easier handling. Salt and pepper to taste. If the nuts are salted, skip the salt.

Beat the egg into the water. Dip the fish pieces into the egg wash and then into the chopped nuts.

Sauté fillets over medium high heat, turning once, until golden brown on both sides.

If you find the nut flavor too dominant, use half bread or cracker crumbs.

Walleye Fillets with Mustard-Dill Sauce

> 2 pounds walleye fillets, skinned, washed and dried. 4 servings.
>
> cooking oil or butter or margarine
>
> salt and pepper to taste
>
> 2 cups flour

> *Mustard-Dill Sauce*
>
> 4 T butter
>
> 4 T flour
>
> 2 cups milk
>
> ⅓ cup dill, chopped fine (or ½ volume dill seed)
>
> 4 T prepared mustard (either yellow or Grey Poupon)

Prepare the sauce by melting the butter in a sauce pan. Stir in the flour. Stir and cook over low heat until it starts to thicken. Add other ingredients, continuing to heat and stir for 2 or 3 minutes. Set sauce aside.

Season the fillets to taste. Dredge in the flour and sauté in butter (or oil) until light brown on both sides (turning once).

Display the fillets on a platter. Spoon a little sauce in the middle of each fillet.

Walleye Nuggets and Zesty Cherry Dipping Sauce

1 pound walleye fillets, skinned, washed and dried. Makes hors d'oeuvres for 6.

½ cup cornmeal
½ t oregano
½ t tarragon
1 cup water
1 egg
oil, butter or margarine for frying

Cherry Dipping Sauce
8 oz. cherry jelly
2 T lemon juice
1 pinch (⅛ t) mace
¼ t ground cloves

Cut fillets into one inch chunks. Combine corn meal, oregano and tarragon.

Beat the egg into the water.

Heat the cooking oil in a skillet. Dip the nuggets in the egg wash and then toss them in the cornmeal mixture, a few at a time, until well coated. Sauté in the skillet in a single layer, turning until brown on all sides. Keep warm.

Prepare the dipping sauce by combining all ingredients in a sauce pan over medium heat. Stir continuously until hot.

Place the nuggets on a plate with a toothpick in each. Place the sauce in a bowl.

A tartar sauce may be substituted for the cherry sauce.

Minnesota Walleye Cakes

1½ pounds walleye fillets, skinned, washed and dried and chopped into small pieces (no more than ¼ inch). Serves 4.

4 slices bread cut into small pieces; do not use crusts

2 eggs

2 T mayonnaise

1 T prepared mustard

1 T horseradish, grated

salt and pepper to taste

4 T butter

Chop the walleye and the bread slices into small pieces.

Mix together all ingredients, thoroughly, for an even distribution.

Mold into 8 hamburger shaped patties. Brown the patties in butter on both sides.

Bake patties on a lightly greased baking sheet in a preheated 350° oven for 8 minutes.

Serve with tartar sauce or on a bun. If served on a bun, onion and/or tomato slices may be added along with some mayonnaise or tartar sauce.

Walleye (Hot or Cold) with Cucumber Sauce

2 pounds walleye fillets, skinned, washed and dried. Serves 4.

salt and pepper to taste

Sauce Ingredients

2 medium cucumbers, peeled and sliced thin (or chopped)

1 T lemon juice

1 T chives, chopped

2 T chopped fresh dill

2 T parsley, chopped

¼ cup white wine

1 cup light cream (or yogurt)

salt and pepper to taste

Place the fillets on a microwave-safe dish. Tuck the tail ends under each fillet so as to have as near even thickness as possible. Season lightly with salt and pepper and microwave about 4 to 5 minutes or until the fish is opaque or can be flaked with a fork.

Prepare sauce in advance by combining all ingredients. Chill ½ hour.

Walleye may be served hot or cold. If fillets are served hot, ask each guest to spoon on the sauce as the fish are eaten so that it will not cool the fillets too much. If served cold, arrange the fish on a platter and spoon the sauce in the center of each piece.

Walleye with Cream and Crumb Topping

2 pounds walleye fillets, skinned, washed and dried. Serves 4.

½ cup white wine

½ cup leeks, chopped (both the white and green parts)

1 cup fish stock* or combine clam juice with chicken broth

1½ cups heavy cream

1½ cups bread crumbs

2 eggs

salt and pepper to taste

cooking oil, butter or margarine

Arrange the fillets or fish pieces on a lightly greased baking sheet in a pre-heated 400° oven. Bake just long enough for fish to become opaque — about 5 or 6 minutes. Do not over-cook.

Topping

Combine fish stock and white wine and cook in a sauce pan over medium heat until reduced by half. Add the cream; bring to a boil until it starts to thicken. Spoon this over the cooked fish (still on the baking sheet).

In a bowl, combine the bread crumbs, chopped leeks, balance of the cream (½ cup) and eggs. Stir in salt and pepper to taste. Sprinkle this topping over the sauce-coated fish pieces.

See pages 87-88.

Place the fish under a broiler just long enough for the topping to brown and begin to puff.

Walleye Fillets with Skins On

This will provide quite a different flavor than skinned fillets. Scale the walleyes before filleting. Most fish markets sell walleyes with the skin still on and already scaled.

> 2 pounds fillets, washed and dried. Serves 4.
> ¼ pound butter
> salt and pepper to taste

Cut the fillets into serving size pieces so that they will lie flat in a skillet. Season both sides with salt and pepper to taste. Melt the butter in the skillet and sauté the fish over medium-high heat, skin side down until the skin is brown and crisp.

Place the fish, skin side up, on a lightly greased baking sheet in a pre-heated 400° oven for about 4 or 5 minutes until the fish flakes with a fork.

Serve with a tartar sauce or mild salsa.

Baked Walleye Fillets on a Bed of Mushrooms

> 2 pounds walleye fillets, skinned, washed and dried. Serves 4.
> 1 pound fresh mushrooms, chopped in fairly large pieces
> 4 T chopped onion
> ½ cup white wine
> ½ cup water
> 1 bay leaf
> 10 peppercorns
> 9 T butter

Step #1: Prepare the mushrooms.
Chop mushrooms into bite-size pieces.
Melt 6 tablespoons of butter.
Sauté ¼ cup chopped onion in the butter (about three minutes)
Add the chopped mushrooms and continue to cook slowly for about 5 minutes.

Set the mushrooms aside until the fillets have been baked. (If fresh mushrooms are not available, you may use pre-cooked, canned mushrooms.)

Step #2: Bake the fillets.

Lay the fillets in a shallow baking dish.

Add ½ cup water, ½ cup white wine, ten whole black peppercorns, and 1 bay leaf.

Bake in a medium oven (350°) for 30 minutes.

Step #3: Prepare a sauce.

Just before removing the fish from the oven, melt 3 tablespoons of butter or margarine. Stir in 3 tablespoons flour while the mixture cooks slowly (for a couple of minutes). Pour the juices off the fillets into the butter-flour mixture— slowly stirring all the while.

When the sauce has thickened, remove from heat and stir in ⅔ cup cream. Season to taste with salt and pepper.

Step #4: Finally—

Cover the bottom of a second baking dish with the mushrooms,

Lay the fillets on this bed of mushrooms.

Cover the fillets with the cream sauce.

Return to a hot oven (450°) for a few minutes until lightly browned.

Garnish and serve.

Walleye and Mushroom Roll-Ups

> 6 walleye fillets (about 2 pounds) serves 4.
>
> 2 cups fresh mushrooms, chopped
>
> 12 slices bacon
>
> 2 T lemon juice
>
> ¼ pound butter
>
> 1 T onion, finely chopped
>
> salt and pepper

Sauté mushrooms and onion in butter until tender. Cut each fillet lengthwise into two long strips. Season lightly with salt and pepper. Scatter the mushrooms and onion pieces uniformly over the twelve strips. Roll up each fillet strip, encircle with bacon strip, and pin with toothpicks.

Broil about 10 minutes each or until fish flakes easily with a fork. Pour a little of the leftover butter and lemon juice mixture over each roll-up before serving.

Fried Walleye Fillets with Cream

2 pounds walleye fillets, skinned, washed and dried. Serves 4.

cooking oil, butter or margarine

1 cup flour

1 cup light cream

3 T chopped chives

2 T parsley, chopped

2 T cooked beets, chopped
(may use pickled beets)

salt and pepper to taste

Season the fillets on both sides, dredge in the flour, and sauté until brown on both sides. Remove to a serving platter.

Add the cream to the same skillet and bring to a boil. Pour the hot cream over the fish pieces. Sprinkle with chopped chives, parsley and beets.

Grilled Walleye on a Bun

1½ pounds walleye fillets, skinned, washed and dried. 4 servings.

1 cup cracker crumbs

cooking oil, butter or margarine

1 cup water

1 egg

8 rolls or hamburger buns

butter or margarine spread

salt and pepper to taste

Other options: lettuce leaves, onion slices, tomato slices, and/or tartar sauce

Cut the fillets into pieces that will fit in the rolls or buns.

For grilling

Spray Pam or other vegetable oil on the grill. Spread softened butter or margarine on the top side of the fish pieces. Season lightly with salt and pepper. Grill until fish is opaque or flakes with a fork (about 5 or 6 minutes).

Or — Try Frying

Beat the egg into the water in a bowl. Place the cracker crumbs in a separate bowl. Season the fish pieces lightly. Dip them first in the egg wash and then in the crumbs. Sauté over medium-high heat until brown on both sides — turning once.

Serve on a roll or bun along with any — or all — of the options listed above.

CHAPTER IV

NORTHERN PIKE

Chad Longbella, Staples, Mn. with two "almost trophy" Lake of the Woods baking-size northern pike.

Long underrated for its culinary qualities because of its difficult bone structure, the northern pike has become more popular in recent years as fishermen have learned to de-bone the fillets. It should also be noted that bones are not a problem when the fish is ground or pickled. Baking, also makes the bones easier to handle.

The pictures which follow show one procedure that works quite well, and even though about 15% of the meat is sacrificed, it is well worth it.

1. Fillet the northern the same as you would a walleye or any other fish. Leave the skin on the fillet until after you have finished the de-boning process.
2. The ridge of meat containing the bones will be visible. Cut an "inverted V" along the sides of this ridge, but not all the way through the fillet, as shown in figure #1.
3. Make a horizontal cut between the ends of the "V" at the large end of the fillet. Now lift the ridge of bones in one strip out of the fillet as you release it with your knife. (figures #2 and #3).
4. Run your finger (carefully) down the cut; if you feel any "Y" bones left—remove them.
5. Skin the fillet.
   Smaller northerns may be deboned—quickly—by cutting off the tail piece (about ¼ of the fillet) which usually has few bones. Then make your "V cuts" all the way through the fillet. With this process it is better to remove the skin before you make the cuts just described. You will end up with two rather long, narrow fillets or "fish sticks," plus the tail piece.
   If the fillets from a large fish are too thick to fry well (especially if you like your fish crisp), try slicing the fillet in two—lengthwise, with a horizontal cut.

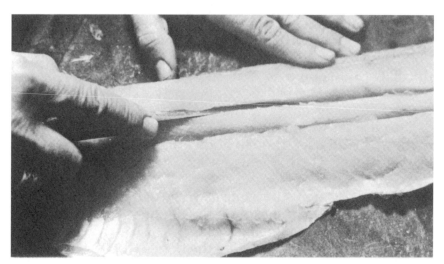

Figure 1. Cut an inverted "V" along the ridge of "Y" bones.

Figure 2. Lifting the ridge of "Y" bones out of the fillet.

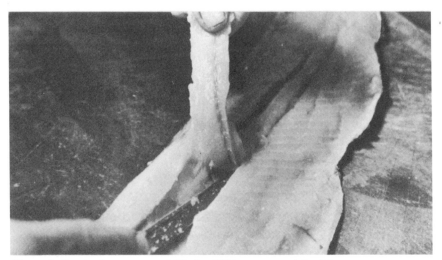
Figure 3. Continuing to cut and lift the "Y" bones out of the fillet.

Whole Northern Baked with Herbs

1 whole northern pike, four pounds live weight or larger, scaled, with head, tail, fins, and entrails removed—washed and dried inside and out. Allow ½ pound dressed weight per serving.

¼ pound butter, melted

2 T lemon juice

6 to 12 sprigs of herbs of your choosing.

With a four pound (live weight) pike use 6 or 7 sprigs. Add the equivalent of one additional sprig per pound for larger fish. Basil, tarragon, dill, parsley and thyme are all possibilities. If you cannot find fresh herbs, use dried or flaked. If all you can have is the powder or minced very fine — use sparingly.

Rub the dressed fish inside and out with the lemon juice* and then brush inside and out with the melted butter. Season to taste with salt and pepper. Add the herbs. Fasten the body cavity closed with wood skewers or use needle and thread. Place the fish in a roasting pan, but lay foil on the bottom first for easier cleaning. If you do not have a large enough pan, you may wrap the entire fish in foil.

Bake in a pre-heated 350° oven allowing 10 minutes for each

inch of thickness. The last 15 minutes, uncover the roaster or open the foil along the back.

Check for doneness by trying the large end of the fish with a fork to see if it will flake.

*If time permits, refrigerate the northern for 2 or 3 hours after you have rubbed it with lemon juice .

Fried Northern Fillets with Herb Seasoning

2 pounds deboned and skinned northern fillets. Serves 4.

vegetable oil, butter or margarine

1 cup cracker or bread crumbs or one of the cornmeal coating mixes* available.

1 T minced or powdered herbs, such as basil, tarragon, dill or thyme. The total of all spices combined should not exceed 1½ tablespoons and go easy on the tarragon.

½ t salt

½ t white pepper

1 large egg

1 cup water

Cut the fillets into serving size pieces, wash and pat dry with paper towel.

In a bowl, thoroughly mix all seasonings and herbs with the crumbs. Beat the egg into the water. Dip each piece of fish into the egg wash and then into the seasoned crumbs.

Sauté over medium-high heat until the fish is opaque and flakes with a fork.

*If a commercial mix is used, it probably already contains a variety of seasonings. Try a piece of fish with just the mix before you consider adding other spices.

Grilled Northern Kabobs

> 1½ pounds skinned, deboned northern pike, cut into 2 inch squares and seasoned lightly with salt and pepper. Serves 4.
> 1 pound large mushrooms
> 2 green peppers cut into chunks
> 1 zucchini squash, sliced thick
> 8 small tomatoes, (cherry size)

> *Basting Sauce*
> ¼ pound butter, melted
> 1 clove garlic, minced
> ½ t Worcestershire sauce
> ½ T lemon

Stir together all ingredients and brush all sides of each chunk of northern pike. Also baste the vegetable pieces.

Poaching Liquid for Mushrooms
> ½ cup white wine
> ½ cup water

Combine water and wine; bring to a boil; poach mushrooms 2 or 3 minutes.

Broiling Process

Place alternately, pieces of fish, mushrooms, green pepper, tomatoes, and zucchini on wire skewers.

Broil over hot coals for about 5 or 6 minutes, turning once, or until fish chunks are opaque.

Northern Nugget Hors d'oeuvres with Sweet and Sour Sauce

> 1 pound deboned, skinned northern fillet. Cut into 1 inch square pieces. Hors d'oeuvres for 4.
> ½ cup crumbs (bread, crackers or commercial mix)
> salt and pepper to taste
> cooking oil, butter or margarine

Season the nuggets, toss them in the crumbs, and sauté them over medium-high heat, turning them so that all are brown on all sides. (If the crumbs do not stick to the nuggets, beat an egg into a cup of water and dip the fish in the egg wash first.)

Sweet and Sour Sauce

¾ cup sugar
½ cup rice wine or cider vinegar
½ cup catsup
½ cup water
juice of 1 lemon
1 t soy sauce
¼ cup cornstarch dissolved in ¼ cup water

Combine sugar, vinegar, catsup, water and lemon juice in a saucepan. Cook over medium heat 3 to 4 minutes. Stir in soy sauce and dissolved cornstarch. Bring to boil, stirring constantly. Cook until thick and clear.

Serve while both the fish and the sauce are warm. Insert a toothpick into each nugget for easier handling.

Creamed Northern with Horseradish Sauce

2 pounds fillets, skinned, deboned and cut into
1½ inch chunks. Serves 4.

1 lemon, sliced
water
1 T salt

Cover the fillet chunks with water, add the lemon slices and salt, and bring to a boil. Fish should flake easily when done (about 15 minutes). Prepare the sauce from the following ingredients:

1 cup light cream
½ cup water in which fish was boiled
3 T butter
2 T flour
2 T grated horseradish

Melt the butter, stir in the flour, add the fish stock and cream. Place the fish chunks in the sauce and bring to a boil briefly. Remove from heat and stir in the grated horseradish. Serve the fish and the sauce over boiled potatoes. Add a generous pat of cold butter to top off each serving.

Fish Soup

1½ pounds deboned northern, cut into one-inch
    cubes. Serves 6.

2 cups milk

3 cups water

½ cup celery, chopped

1 medium onion, sliced (pick apart the slices)

3 large potatoes, diced (bite-size chunks)

10 peppercorns

1 bay leaf

½ T salt

½ stick butter (⅛ pound)

1 T flour

Start with the 3 cups of water in a kettle; add the potatoes and bring to a boil. After boiling for 3 or 4 minutes, add the fish, salt, whole black peppers, onion and celery and continue at a slow boil until potatoes can be easily pierced with a fork.

Mix the tablespoon of flour into the milk until smooth. Reduce heat to "simmer". Add the flour-milk mixture to the soup and stir until thoroughly blended. Add butter a little at a time and continue heat until butter is melted (about 5 minutes).

Poached Northern

2 pounds northern pike fillets, skinned and
    deboned, cut into 3-inch pieces.

2 quarts water

½ cup white vinegar (preferably wine vinegar)

1 large onion, sliced

1 stalk celery, cut into chunks

2 T minced parsley

12 peppercorns

1 bay leaf

1 T salt

Combine all ingredients in a cooking pot, except the fish. Bring to a boil and then reduce heat and let simmer for 1 hour.

Add fish pieces and increase heat slightly so that it begins to boil. Fish is done when it is opaque. (5 to 10 minutes).

Serve fish with melted butter. Discard poaching solution and ingredients.

Lake Superior Northern Pike Chowder

2 pounds deboned, skinned fillets cut into 1 inch chunks. Serves 6.

1 large green pepper, sliced and cut into pieces about 1 inch long

1 large onion, sliced and broken into circles

1 cup celery, diced, $\frac{1}{2}$ inch chunks

2 cloves garlic, minced

1 - 10$\frac{1}{2}$ oz. cn. tomato soup

1 - #2 cn. stewed tomatoes

2 cups tomato juice

1 - 14 oz. cn. evaporated milk

1 chicken bouillon cube, crushed

1 t tarragon

3 bay leaves

$\frac{1}{2}$ t white pepper

$\frac{1}{8}$ pound butter

Sauté the green pepper, onion, celery and garlic in the butter until the onion is translucent. (4 or 5 minutes).

Combine all the ingredients in a 3 quart sauce pan (except for the fish) and bring to a boil. Reduce heat and let simmer uncovered — about 15 minutes. Add northern pieces and continue to cook for about 10 minutes or until the fish is opaque.

Ground Northern Patties

> 2 pounds northern fillets, skinned, but need not be deboned. Serves 6.
>
> 2 eggs
>
> salt and pepper
>
> cooking oil or butter or margarine
>
> tartar sauce
>
> lettuce
>
> onion and tomato slices (one of each per patty)
>
> hamburger buns

Run the fillets through a meat grinder (fine setting). If bones may still be seen in the ground meat, run the fish through the grinder again.

Beat the eggs, lightly, and then stir them thoroughly into the ground northern.

Mold into hamburger-size patties. Season with salt and pepper to taste.

Fry in light oil (or butter or margarine) over medium-high heat, turning once so that the patties are well-browned on both sides.

Serve on buns with guest's choice of combinations of tartar sauce, lettuce, onion and tomato.

Ruby's * Pickled Fish

Fillet, skin and cut into small pieces. Place in a large crock and add ⅝ cup of salt for each quart of cut up fish. Cover fish with cider vinegar.

Let stand 4 to 6 days at 40° temperature. Rinse fish and let stand in cold water ½ hour. Pack loosely in jars, adding onion slices over each layer of fish. Cover with the following cold pickle solution:

> 1 qt. distilled vinegar
>
> 1 pound sugar
>
> ½ box or ⅝ oz. pickling spice

Seal jars and let stand one week (refrigerated) before using.

Ruby's Fish Balls

Use large northerns or similar fish.

Fillet out and skin slabs and grind-up. Grind a few raw potatoes and a little onion with the fish.

Mix in a little cracker crumbs, a couple of eggs, a little sweet cream and salt and pepper to taste. Add enough flour so that fish can be made into balls (about the size of beef meatballs). Brown in butter in a skillet. Then pour cream over the fish balls and gently stir until it has the look and consistency of meatballs and gravy.

*courtesy Ruby Treloar, Deerwood, Mn., Hostess at Ruttgers on Bay Lake, master chef.

Three Favorite Stuffed Northern Pike Recipes by Max Ruttger III*

All three recipes call for placing the stuffing between pieces of northern approximately 3" by 6". In each case begin by deboning enough fillets to make twelve pieces of that size. It should be noted that pieces smaller than 3" x 6" can be used to make the top layer of fish, so nothing need be wasted.

For each recipe, lay six pieces of fish in a baking dish and sprinkle with seasoned salt.

Recipe #1: Northern stuffed with vegetables — serves 6.

6 medium carrots

3 medium zucchini

3 T butter

3 cloves garlic, minced

seasoned salt

Shred carrots and zucchini; sauté until slightly soft in the butter and minced garlic. Sprinkle with seasoned salt and toss while cooking.

Place a layer of cooked vegetable mixture over each of the six pieces of fish in the baking dish. Cover with the remaining pieces of fish. Sprinkle top layer with seasoned salt. Bake at 350° about 30 minutes, covered.

Serve as is or top with hollandaise sauce.

Recipe #2: Northern stuffed with Spinach — serves 6.

2 bunches fresh spinach
2 T butter
1 clove garlic, minced
¼ cup parmesan cheese
¾ cup sour cream
¾ cup fine breadcrumbs

Wash spinach and discard stems. Melt butter in large sauce pan or skillet. Add minced garlic. Add spinach, tossing until wilted. Stir in parmesan, sour cream and breadcrumbs.

Place a layer of spinach mixture on each of the six pieces of northern in the baking dish. Cover with the remaining six pieces. Bake covered for about 30 minutes at 350°.

Recipe #3: Northern stuffed with smoked salmon

1 lb. smoked salmon
1 - 8 oz. pkg. cream cheese
2 T lemon juice
2 T horseradish
seasoned salt

Soften cream cheese. Add lemon juice, horseradish and flaked smoked salmon. Blend thoroughly. Place a layer of the smoked salmon mixture over each of the six pieces of northern in the baking dish. Top with the remaining pieces of fish.

If desired, top with mornay sauce before baking.

Bake covered in a 350° oven for about 30 minutes.

If sauce is used, remove covering last 10-15 minutes to allow top to brown.

Mornay Sauce — makes 2 cups

4 T butter
4 T flour
1 t seasoned salt
1 t nutmeg
1½ cups milk
½ cup dry white wine
½ cup grated Swiss cheese

Melt butter; add flour, salt and nutmeg. Cook over low heat until bubbly. Blend in milk and wine. Cook, whisking until thickened. Add cheese and whisk until cheese melts.

*Courtesy Max Ruttger III, Brainerd attorney, master chef

CHAPTER V

MUSKIES

Jeff Cowie, Dover, New Hampshire, with a baking-size muskie from Canadian waters

With the possible exception of trophy size wall-hangers, muskies are meant to be released. Not that muskies aren't good eating—they are, but they are a relatively rare fish, hard to catch and among the most spectacular of fighters. A released muskie will give others the same matchless thrill.

But what should you do with that rare legal fish with the giant lure hopelessly imbedded in its throat or fatally damaged in the fight? Keep it and bake it.

These recipes also work well with northern pike.

Muskie with Raisin Stuffing

Preparing the fish: Scale and gut the fish; remove the head, tail and all fins. Wash and dry the fish, inside and out.

Score the back of the fish with cross-section cuts about three inches apart—down to the backbone.

Salt and pepper, inside and out and in the cuts.

Preparing the stuffing:

>1 cup raisins
>
>¼ lb. butter (added to one cup hot water)
>
>2 cups croutons or dry breadcrumbs
>
>1 large onion, chopped but not too fine
>
>salt and pepper
>
>1 cup chopped bologna (or wieners or polish sausage or luncheon meat)

Place the croutons, raisins, meat and onions in a bowl. Salt and pepper lightly while stirring the ingredients together.

Add and stir in the butter-hot water mixture just before stuffing the fish. Do not stuff fish until you are ready to bake it.

Lay a sheet of foil on the bottom of the roaster.

Stuff the fish (loosely) and place upright on the sheet of foil.

Fold the foil up along both sides of the fish—do not cover the back. The foil will hold in the stuffing. If your fish is too long for the roaster, you may cut it in two and bake the two sections side by side.

Leftover stuffing or additional stuffing may be baked in a foil package alongside the fish or even outside the roaster.

Place a strip of bacon and a slice of onion, alternately, over each score (or cut).

Cover the roaster and place in a preheated, 300° oven. After one hour, remove cover and continue to bake until the meat may be flaked easily from the backbone (as viewed from the end of the fish).

Transfer the baked fish to a platter. Cut through the backbone at each score mark, separating the fish into serving-size portions. The stuffing may be lifted out with each portion as it is served.

Serve with tartar sauce and/or lemon.

Lemon Rubbed and Wine-Basted Baked Fish With Wild Rice Dressing

Choose a large northern pike, muskie, salmon, lake trout or whitefish. Scale and draw the fish. Remove head, tail and fins; wash thoroughly inside and out and dry.

Strain the juice of three lemons; salt lightly. Rub the inside and the outside of the fish—thoroughly—with the salted lemon juice. Refrigerate the fish for two or three hours.

Prepare Stuffing:

> 1 cup wild rice, washed (will make three cups cooked rice)*
>
> ½ cup melted butter or margarine mixed with ½ cup hot water
>
> 1 large onion, chopped
>
> ⅓ pound chopped bologna, summer sausage or polish sausage or luncheon meat (optional)
>
> 1 cup celery, chopped
>
> 1 small green pepper (or ⅓ cup)

Cook the wild rice:

3 cups of water

1 cup wild rice (washed)

salt and pepper

¼ lb. melted butter or margarine

Season water with one tablespoon salt and bring to a boil. Add rice and lower the heat so that the water just simmers. Cook—covered—for about 45 minutes or until the kernels are well opened and the rice is tender. Do not overcook.

Pour off any water that has not been absorbed. Add pepper and a little more salt to taste; pour on the melted butter, and fluff with a fork.

Sauté the celery and onions:

Cook slowly in butter or margarine for about three minutes or until the onions are translucent and the celery is light brown.

Combine:

The wild rice, onion, celery, chopped meat, and green pepper. Season lightly with salt and pepper. Pour ½ cup melted butter combined with an equal amount of hot water over the mixture and stir the ingredients together—thoroughly.

Stuff and bake:

Pat the chilled fish dry and stuff loosely, just before you place it in the oven. Leftover dressing may be baked separately in foil alongside the fish. Place a sheet of foil in the bottom of a roaster, then place the fish in the roaster (back up). Bring the foil up halfway around the fish to hold in the stuffing. Place in a pre-heated medium oven (350°).

Melt ¼ pound of butter and add an equal amount of white wine. Baste fish from time to time with the wine-butter mixture.

Bake until the meat flakes easily from the large end of the fish (about 15 to 20 minutes per pound).

Transfer baked fish to serving platter; garnish with parsley and serve with lemon wedges.

*You may substitute 1 cup raisins for the wild rice and add 1 ½ cups croutons. You may prefer to use half white and half wild rice.

Charcoal Baked Whole Fish

Scale the fish. Cut off the head, tail and fins. When you draw the fish, make a single cut down the center of the stomach so that the body cavity will hold as much stuffing as possible.

Prepare your favorite dressing—or try this one:

   3 cups croutons or dry breadcrumbs
   1 large onion, chopped
   1 cup celery, chopped
   1 small can mushrooms, sliced
   $\frac{1}{4}$ pound (1 stick) margarine or butter, melted
   $\frac{1}{2}$ cup hot water

If croutons are not seasoned or if you use breadcrumbs, season with salt and pepper and $\frac{1}{2}$ teaspoon sage and/or poultry seasoning.

Sauté the onion in the butter or margarine; when the onion is translucent (but not brown), add the $\frac{1}{2}$ cup hot water. Place the croutons (or breadcrumbs) and chopped celery in a bowl. Pour the butter-water-onion mixture over the contents and mix well. Add seasoning—evenly.

Stuff the body cavity just before baking. Sew up the fish. Extra dressing may be prepared by wrapping it in foil and placing it alongside the fish on the grill.

Place the fish on its side on a well-oiled charcoal grill (over pre-ignited charcoal that has turned gray, thus indicating it is ready). If your grill has a cover, baking should take about 8 minutes per pound. Without a cover it will take about twice as long and you must turn the fish when it is about half done. You may check doneness by using a fork to see if the meat will flake easily around the exposed backbone at the large end of the fish. Baste from time to time with melted butter.

To avoid flames burning the fish, place a piece of foil directly under the fish and bank the charcoal on each side of the foil.

CHAPTER VI

SALMON

Bruce Lund, Staples, and Greg Johnson, St. Cloud,
with three 40 to 50 pound King Salmon from
Alaska's Kenai River.

Salmon recipes are included in this freshwater fish cookbook because so many are now being caught in our inland lakes where they have been planted. What a great addition to freshwater fishing and to the dinner tables of Mid-America!

Marv's* Three Zesty Baked Salmon Recipes

All three of these recipes are for oven baked fillets. Remove the skin from the fillets, wash and pat dry and then cut into serving size pieces. Cuts should not exceed ¾ inch in thickness. If the salmon is large and the fillets are thicker than this, cut each of the fillets into two fillets with a horizontal cut starting where the fillet starts to get thicker than ¾ inch. This will give you 4 fillets per fish; cut into serving size pieces.

Use a baking sheet, sprayed or coated with cooking oil. As you place the cuts on the baking sheet, be sure the sides do not touch each other. Pre-heat the oven to 300° and place the tray in the center of the oven. Bake for a total of 20 minutes.

Recipe #1
Season the fish with salt, lemon pepper and dill weed (sparingly).
Spread regular mayonnaise over the fish (about 1 level T per piece).
Sprinkle very lightly with parsley flakes.

Recipe #2
Season cuts with salt, lemon pepper and a trace of sugar.
Cover each cut with *mild* salsa sauce.

Recipe #3
Season lightly with salt, lemon pepper and dill weed (sparingly).
Prepare a mixture of 1 stick butter (melted) and 1 T Worcestershire sauce.
Bake fish for 5 minutes, then baste with the sauce.
Bake another 10 minutes, and again baste with the sauce from the pan. Cook an additional 5 minutes.

*Marvin Campbell, Brainerd, Minnesota, Retired banker; master chef.

Sauces for Salmon

Alaskan Barbecue Sauce*
May be used on fillets or whole fish while they are broiling and/or when the fish is served. Designed for salmon but works very well with lake trout or northern pike. It also works miracles for catfish or bullheads!

Ingredients for 2 pounds of fillets or steaks:

    ½ pound butter

    1 lg. clove garlic, diced

    4 T soy sauce

    2 T mustard

    ¼ cup catsup

    dash Worcestershire sauce

Using a double broiler, melt the butter. Stir in all the other ingredients and continue heating for about 20 minutes, stirring occasionally. Brush part of the liquid on the fillets or steaks while they are broiling and serve the balance (hot) with the meal. The above recipe will be sufficient to use with four servings.

*courtesy Mary Hayenga, St. Cloud, Mn.

Dill Sauce
Ingredients for approximately 4 pounds fillets or a 6 pound baked fish (live weight):

    2 T minced fresh dill or 1 T dry dill

    1 T chopped onion

    2 T butter

    1 T flour

    ½ cup cream

    1 cup fish stock*

    salt and pepper to taste

Sauté the onion pieces until clear. Stir in flour and cook for 3 minutes. Stir in all other ingredients, seasoning to taste. Serve hot over fillets, steaks or baked fish.

*see pages 87,88 and 89

Broiling Sauce for Basting

Baste fillets on the grill with a mixture of soy sauce and melted butter. Use proportions of 2 T soy sauce to ¼ pound melted butter.

Salmon Salad

1½ pounds (6 pieces) salmon fillet (skinned), serves 6.

2 cloves garlic, minced

3 T lemon juice

½ cup olive oil

1 t salt

1 head lettuce, torn into pieces (salad size)

1 cup salsa sauce

¼ pound butter (to sauté fish)

Cut the salmon fillets into 6 serving size pieces. Use fillets from smaller salmon or cut a thick fillet from a larger salmon into 2 fillets (horizontal cut the length of the fillet).

Prepare marinade by mixing together the garlic, lemon juice, salt and olive oil. Place the fillets in a shallow, flat dish and pour ½ of the marinade over the pieces. Refrigerate, covered, about 30 minutes. Discard this marinade.

Remove the fish and sauté in butter a few minutes on each side until done.

Arrange the lettuce on 6 salad plates. Lay the fish cuts (hot or cold) on the lettuce. Drizzle the other half of the marinade over the fish and lettuce. Spoon salsa sauce (about 2 T per serving) over the fish.

Smoked Salmon Dip

1 pound smoked salmon, flaked (if flakes are very large, chop into smaller pieces.)

1 cup mayonnaise

½ t Worcestershire sauce

1 clove garlic, minced

2 T celery, chopped fine

2 T onions, chopped fine

3 T sweet pickle relish

Mix thoroughly and refrigerate before serving.

Salmon and Cucumber Spread or Dip

½ pound cooked, flaked salmon (chop if flakes are too large).

½ cup mayonnaise

½ cup cucumbers, chopped fine

¼ t white pepper

Mix thoroughly and refrigerate.

Curried Salmon Dip

1 pound cooked salmon, flaked (and chopped if flakes are large)

1 pound yogurt (plain)

½ cup mayonnaise

4 T chives or onion greens chopped fine

1 T curry powder

2 T chutney

1 t white pepper

Mix thoroughly and refrigerate.

Salmon - Dill Spread

½ pound salmon, pre-cooked and flaked (chopped if flakes are large)

½ pound cream cheese

2 T lemon or lime juice

½ t white pepper

dash of salt

1 T dill weed

3 T mayonnaise

Use as sandwich spread or on small pieces of bread or crackers as appetizers.

Baked Salmon

Try any of the baking recipes for northern pike, muskie or lake trout.

CHAPTER VII
LAKE TROUT

Kevin Crocker, Big Lake, Mn. and Dr. Chris Longbella, Chippewa Falls, Wi., with four Canadian Lake Trout

Almost any of the salmon recipes are appropriate for Lake trout — and visa versa.

Charcoal Broiled Fillets (or gas grill)

2 pounds lake trout fillets, cut into serving size pieces (leave skin on). Serves 4.
season lightly with lemon pepper

basting sauce
¼ pound butter, melted
1 T Worcestershire sauce
½ t dill weed

Place fillets, skin side down, on an oiled grill over ignited (gray) coals or gas flame.

Combine the melted butter, Worcestershire sauce and dill weed. Baste the fish 2 or 3 times while broiling (depends on thickness of fillet).

Cover while cooking.

Fish will be done when it flakes easily at the thickest end.

Whole Lake Trout on the Grill with Cashew Stuffing

1 lake trout, 5 pounds or larger, dressed
½ cup lime (or lemon) juice

Lubricate the fish well with the juice, inside and out. Refrigerate 3 to 4 hours (depending on the size of the fish).

cashew stuffing
2 cups seasoned croutons
1½ cups cashews
½ cup celery, diced
½ large onion, chopped
½ t nutmeg
¼ pound butter, melted
½ cup hot water
½ t garlic salt

Season the melted butter with the garlic salt. Sauté the onion and celery in the butter until the onions are translucent. Place all of the dry ingredients in a bowl. Pour the butter-onion-celery mixture over the dry ingredients in the bowl. Stir in the hot water and mix thoroughly.

Stuff and sew-up the trout. Leftover stuffing may be wrapped in foil and also cooked on the grill. (Do not stuff the fish until you are ready to put it on the grill.)

Lay the stuffed fish on a well oiled grill over ignited (gray) coals. Cover and bake until the fish flakes very easily on the large end of the trout. Allow about 8 to 10 minutes a pound, depending on the heat.

Sauces for Lake Trout

Sherry Cream Sauce
Ingredients for about 2 pounds of fish, serves 4.

> 1 cup chicken broth, heated (milk may be substituted)
> 3 t flour
> ⅛ t pepper
> ½ t salt
> 3 T butter
> ½ cup heavy cream
> 2 T sherry

Melt the butter. Remove from heat and stir in flour, salt and pepper. Blend in hot broth. Return to heat and cook (stir regularly) until thick. Stir in cream and sherry.

Serve over sautéed, broiled or baked fish.

Seasoned Wine Sauce
Serve over poached, baked or broiled fish. A French recipe.
Ingredients for about 2 pounds of fillets. (Serves 4)

> 2 cups sparkling wine (or champagne)
> 2 cups heavy cream
> 1½ cups fish stock*
> 1 small onion, minced (or chives or green onion)
> 2 T lemon juice
> ¼ cup chopped parsley
> ½ stick butter (⅛ pound)

Cook the wine and onion in a saucepan over medium heat until the liquid is reduced to about ⅓ cup. Stir in the fish stock and boil about 5 minutes. Add the cream and continue boiling until about 2 cups remain. Reduce heat and add butter one pat at a time. When it is all melted, stir in the parsley and lemon juice.

*see pages 87, 88, 89 and 90.

Hot Basting Sauce

Use for basting and serve the balance of the sauce over grilled or baked lake trout.

Ingredients for 3 pounds steak or 6 pounds whole salmon, serves 6.

1 T butter, melted
1 cup fish stock*
1 small onion, chopped
2 T minced garlic
1 can Italian style tomatoes
1 small green or red pepper, chopped
1 T chopped basil or other favorite herb
1 T parsley, chopped
4 drops Tabasco sauce

Sauté the onion and garlic in the butter. Add all other ingredients. Stir and cook over low heat until about ⅓ of the liquid has evaporated.

*see pages 87, 88, 89 and 90.

Flaked Trout Casserole

Poach 1 pound of lake trout fillet until the fish can be easily flaked with a fork.

Ingredients to serve 4:

> Flaked trout from 1 pound fillet (a little over 1 cup)
>
> 1 cup mushrooms, sliced
>
> 1 can mushroom soup
>
> $\frac{1}{8}$ pound butter
>
> 1 - 3 oz. pkg. cream cheese
>
> 1 T chopped onion
>
> 1 T table mustard
>
> $\frac{1}{4}$ cup milk
>
> 2 T pimientos
>
> 1 cup cooked macaroni (See directions on the package.)
>
> $\frac{1}{2}$ cup breadcrumbs

Sauté the mushrooms and onion in the butter. Remove, but save the melted butter.

Soften the cheese and blend into the soup—using a blender or mixer. Stir in the flaked trout, onion, mustard, macaroni, milk, mushrooms, and pimientos.

Pour mixture into a casserole. Mix crumbs and melted butter and sprinkle on top.

Bake in a medium oven (350°) for 25 minutes.

Fish and Potato Casserole

> 2 pounds of trout fillets, cut into serving size pieces. Serves 4.
>
> 6 potatoes, sliced
>
> butter, enough to butter the casserole dish
>
> 3 T chopped dill or $1\frac{1}{2}$ T dill seed
>
> salt and pepper
>
> 6 eggs
>
> 1 pint of milk (2 cups)

Butter the casserole dish. Place a layer of sliced potatoes

on the bottom. Next a layer of fillets. Lightly season the fillets with salt and pepper. Sprinkle lightly with the dill. Add another layer of potatoes; then a layer of fish, more seasonings, etc. making sure the top layer is potatoes. Beat the eggs and milk together and pour over all. Bake in a low oven (250°) for about 1 hour or until potatoes are done.

Great Slave Lake Guides' Recipe for Shore Lunch

2 pounds lake trout fillets, skinned, washed and patted dry, serves 4.

> 1½ cups flour in a heavy-duty paper bag
> 1 t salt
> 1 t pepper
> 2 eggs
> 1½ cups water
> ½ cup cooking oil (they usually use a
>   solid shortening)

Cut trout into serving size portions.

Thoroughly shake the flour, salt and pepper together in the paper bag.

Mix the egg and water together in a bowl.

Shake two or three cuts of fish at a time in the bag with the seasoned flour until well coated.

Dip into the egg wash and then fry in plenty of oil in an iron skillet over a hot fire — turning once — until golden brown on both sides.

Marinated and Fried Lake Trout

2 pounds skinned lake trout fillets, serves 4.

> *marinade*
> 3 T olive oil
> 4 T white wine
> 1 T lemon juice
> 1 onion slice thin and broken into rings
> dash of salt and white pepper

Cut fish into serving size portions and place in a shallow flat dish. Combine all marinade ingredients and pour over fish. Refrigerate 30 minutes. Discard marinade.

Prepare your favorite batter or use a "complete" pancake mix. Just add water but make the batter a little thinner than you would use for pancakes.

Fry in a heavy skillet in a fair amount of oil, butter or margarine. The heavier the batter the more oil you will need. Turn once; fry until brown on both sides. If you prefer, use a deep fryer in which the fish pieces will float in the oil. Do not over-cook.

Ceviche*

50-70 pieces or 3-6 lbs. of Trout or any oily fish. Cut fish in strips ½" wide x 1" to 2" long.

> 1 pint of white vinegar
>
> 2 bottles (8 oz. each) lime juice
>
> 2 medium size onions, sliced thinly
>
> 6 bay leaves
>
> 1 diced tomato
>
> whole peppercorns (30 kernels)
>
> ½ t ground red pepper
>
> few whole little red peppers (small hot chillies)
>
> Tabasco - dash or so
>
> plenty of salt

Place in a crock and refrigerate 48 hours before serving.

*courtesy Mrs. George Cook, Hackensack, Mn.

CHAPTER VIII

STREAM TROUT

Trophy Eastern Brook Trout (4 and 4½ pounds) Goose Bay, Laborador, caught by the author and Dr. Chris Longbella, Chippewa Falls, Wi.

"Stream trout" includes such varieties as speckled (brook), rainbow, brown, cutthroat and Dolly Varden.

The smaller stream trout are so full of flavor they are best prepared with minimal seasonings or use of sauces. Just season lightly, coat with flour or crumbs and sauté in butter. If they are 10 inches or less, fry them whole.

The larger trout, one pound and larger, may be enhanced by any of the following treatments:

Trout Amandine

A restaurant favorite; here's how they do it:

4 trout fillets or smaller whole trout, serves 4.

> flour and salt
> ½ cup butter
> ½ t onion juice
> ¼ cup blanched, finely slivered almonds
> 1 T lemon juice

Wash and dry the fish. Dust with salt and flour. Heat half the butter and onion juice in a heavy skillet and cook fish until lightly browned. Remove and place on a hot serving dish. Pour off the grease remaining in the pan and add the rest of the butter. Add the almonds and brown slowly, then add lemon juice and when it foams, pour it over the fish.

Poached Trout

Use the poaching liquids on pages 87 & 88, or try this one:

1½ pounds dressed trout, cut into 2 inch chunks, serves 4.

(Small trout may be dressed and poached whole.)

> poaching liquid
> 2 cups water
> 1 onion, sliced and separated into rings
> 1 cup celery, cut into ½ inch chunks
> 1 stalk dill (or ½ t dill seed)
> 1 T salt
> 8 peppercorns

Place the poaching ingredients in a skillet or pot small

enough so that the liquid will completely cover the fish pieces. Bring to a boil, then reduce heat and let simmer 10 minutes. Add the fish; bring to a boil again, then reduce heat and let simmer 6 to 10 minutes or until the fish is done.

If you would like to serve with a sauce, try one of those suggested on pages 29 or 42. Or, just dip the pieces in melted butter.

Grilled Trout with Herbs

> 4 - 1 pound trout (live weight), serves 4.
>
> 2 T olive oil
>
> salt and pepper to taste
>
> 4 small sprigs dill
>
> 4 small sprigs rosemary (or other herb)
>
> 4 bay leaves, broken into 3 or 4 pieces

Dress the trout but leave whole. Rub outsides of fish with the olive oil. Season lightly inside and out. Place 1 sprig of each herb and 3 or 4 pieces of bay leaf in the cavity of each fish.

Place on a pre-heated, well-oiled grill. Broil about 8 minutes per side, turning once (or until fish is done).

Smoked Whole Trout

> 4 - 1 pound (live weight) trout, serves 4.
>
> 2 double handfuls of hardwood chips
>   (preferably mesquite)
>
> 2 T olive oil
>
> 1 t thyme
>
> 1 t rosemary
>
> salt and pepper to taste

Dress the trout and rub them (outsides only) with olive oil. Pre-soak the wood chips (30 minutes).

Season the fish inside and out with salt and pepper.

When the charcoal is ready (gray in color), throw the wet woodchips onto the charcoal.

Place the fish, cavity opening down, on a well oiled grill. Cover and cook until the fish flakes easily at the large ends.

Microwave Trout

Dress a one pound trout per person. (Leave on head and tail but gut and wash). Rub inside and out with lemon wedge; season lightly with salt and pepper. Lay in baking dish and cover head and thinner part with foil (providing foil may be used in your microwave). Cover with plastic; vent a few places with a fork.

About six minutes will cook one trout; add about three minutes for each additional fish.

Garnish with parsley and serve with lemon wedges and/or tartar sauce.

CHAPTER IX

PERCH

Long scorned by fishermen as "those pesty little bait stealers", perch in recent years have finally earned the respect due them on the dinner table. As first cousins of the walleye, they are among the most palatable of all freshwater species. Any perch close to a ½ pound, or more, is well worth saving.

Baked Perch with Pecan Crust

 2 pounds perch fillets, skinned, serves 4.
 1 cup breadcrumbs
 1 cup pecans, chopped
 ¼ pound butter, melted
 salt and lemon pepper to taste
 cooking oil, butter or margarine

Arrange the fillets on a well oiled baking sheet. Season with salt and lemon pepper. Sprinkle generously with breadcrumbs and chopped pecans. Drizzle the melted butter over the crumbs.

Bake in a preheated, 300° oven for about 15 minutes or until the crumbs are a crusty brown.

Perch with Parsley and Dill

9 large perch, dressed (scale and remove heads, tails and fins; and drain), serves 3.

Cover bottom of baking dish with ¼ cup finely chopped parsley and arrange the fish in the baking dish.

Top with:

> 2 T finely chopped parsley
> 2 T chopped fresh dill or
> 1 t dill weed

Pour ¼ cup hot water around the fish. Bake at 350° for 20 to 25 minutes and serve.

Cheese-Coated Perch

> 2 pounds fresh perch fillets, serves 4.
> ¼ cup all purpose flour
> 1 beaten egg
> 1 t salt
> dash pepper
> ¼ cup fine dry breadcrumbs
> ¼ cup grated Parmesan cheese
> ¼ cup shortening
> 1 eight ounce can tomato sauce
> ½ t sugar
> ½ t dried basil leaves, crushed

Cut fish into serving size portions. Coat with flour and dip into a mixture of egg, salt and pepper, then dip into a mixture of breadcrumbs and cheese. Fry fish slowly in a skillet or hot shortening until browned on one side. Turn and brown other side. Combine tomato sauce, ¼ cup water, sugar and basil in a saucepan. Simmer 10 minutes and serve with the fish.

Perch Tempura

> 2 lbs. perch fillets, salted to taste, serves 4.
> 1 lemon, halved
> ½ Tempura Batter recipe
> 1 qt. vegetable oil

Cut fish fillets into bite-sized pieces and drain well on paper toweling. Season with salt and squeeze lemon juice over the fish.

Tempura Batter
2 cups sifted flour
3 egg yolks
2 cups ice water

Sift the flour 3 times. Combine the egg yolks and water in a large bowl over ice and beat with a whisk until well blended. Add the flour gradually, stirring and turning the mixture from the bottom with a spoon. Do not overmix. The flour should be visible on top of the batter. Keep the batter over ice while dipping and frying.

Spear pieces of fish and dip in the batter, drain slightly and fry in oil heated to 360° for about 5 minutes, turning to brown evenly.

Perch Stew

1 pound perch fillets, skinned and cut into 2 inch chunks, serves 4.

3 tomatoes, cut into ½ inch chunks
2 cloves garlic, minced
1 medium zucchini, sliced thin (¼")
½ cup chopped celery
1 onion, chopped coarse
1 cup potatoes pre-cooked (but still fairly hard) and sliced
3 carrots, pre-cooked (but still fairly hard) and sliced
1 bay leaf
oil, butter or margarine
1 cup white wine
3 cups water
salt and white pepper to taste
½ cup parsley flakes (for garnish)

Sauté the onion, celery, garlic and zucchini until the onion is translucent. Add the water, wine and tomato pieces and bring to a boil. Reduce heat and let simmer 5 minutes. Add all other ingredients (except parsley) and again bring to a boil. Reduce heat and let simmer 5 minutes or until the perch is done. Serve in bowls: Garnish with parsley flakes.

If the stew is too thin for your preference, use less water.

CHAPTER X

CATFISH AND BULLHEADS

Although spurned by some fishermen in Canada and the northern tier of states, catfish and their smaller cousins, the bullheads, are nation-wide, among the most popular varieties for eating. This has become especially true in recent years as more and more of these fish have been grown commercially. Although the recipes which follow may be used for either variety, they are two distinct species with quite different tastes. Recipes in this book for salmon and trout may work somewhat better for bullheads, and recipes for white-meated fish may work a little better for catfish. Those recipes which follow will work for either, however.

Cheesy Fillets

2 pounds fillets. Serves 4.
1 cup cracker or breadcrumbs
½ cup Parmesan cheese, grated
salt and pepper to taste
cooking oil, butter or margarine
1 egg
1 cup water

Season the fillets (skinned) lightly.
Combine the egg and the water.
Combine the crumbs and cheese in a bowl.
Dip the fillets into the egg wash, then the crumb-cheese

mixture, and fry in a well-oiled griddle over medium high heat. Turn once and fry until a golden brown on both sides.

Fillets with Salsa

2 pounds fillets, skinned. Serves 4.
4 T butter, melted
1 T Worcestershire sauce
1 cup salsa

Broil the fillets on a well oiled grill. Baste two or three times with a mixture of the butter and Worcestershire sauce. Turn once and remove from heat when done (fish flakes easily with a fork).

Serve with the salsa sauce. Remember, salsa may be mild or hot according to your own taste.

Fried in Cornmeal and Served with Hush Puppies

2 pounds skinned fillets. Serves 4.
$\frac{1}{4}$ cup flour
$\frac{3}{4}$ cup cornmeal
salt and pepper to taste
enough oil for deep frying

Cut fillets into serving size pieces.

Season the cuts to taste. Combine the cornmeal and flour. Coat the fillets with the flour-cornmeal mixture. Fry, a few pieces at a time, in hot oil (375°) until golden brown. Do not over-cook. About 5 minutes is usually enough.

Hush Puppies
2 cups self rising white corn meal
1 small onion, chopped fine
$\frac{1}{4}$ cup green pepper, chopped fine
1 egg, beaten
$\frac{3}{4}$ cup milk

Combine corn meal, sugar, green pepper, and onion in a bowl. Combine milk and egg and stir into the ingredients in the bowl.

Drop large tablespoons of dough into hot fat (375°) and let fry until a golden brown.

Fillets with Herbs and Parmesan Cheese in Microwave

2 pounds skinned fillets. Serves 4.

¾ cup Parmesan cheese, grated

1 t oregano

1 t basil

1 t thyme

2 T parsley flakes

Season the fillets evenly with the herbs. Sprinkle with the Parmesan. Add the parsley flakes last.

Cook in microwave until fish flakes with a fork at larger end. If the tail pieces are much thinner than the large end of the fillets, fold the tails under so that the fillets are as even in thickness as possible.

Blackened Fillets

2 pounds skinned fillets. Serves 4.

¼ pound butter, melted

1 t oregano

1 t basil

1 t garlic powder

1 t salt

2 t white pepper

Cut the fillets into serving size pieces. Heat a heavy skillet until it is sizzling hot (about 10 minutes over high heat). Meanwhile, combine the spices in a bowl and mix thoroughly. Dip the cuts into the melted butter and sprinkle the seasoning on each side of the cuts, using about 1 t per side. Place the fish in the hot skillet; drizzle a little of the remaining butter over each. If the skillet is hot enough, about 2 minutes on each side should be enough.

Baked with Tomato Sauce

2 pounds skinned fillets. Serves 4.

1 eight ounce can tomato sauce

2 T salad oil

1 t cheese-garlic salad dressing mix or Italian
     salad dressing mix

½ t salt

Grated Parmesan cheese

Place fish in a greased shallow baking pan. Combine tomato sauce, salad oil, dressing mix and salt. Pour sauce over and around fish. Sprinkle with Parmesan cheese. Bake at 350° for about 40 minutes until fish flakes easily.

Baked in Wine

4 - 1 pound fish (live weight). Serves 4.

1 cup white wine

salt and pepper to taste

4 T paprika

1 lemon, thinly sliced for garnish

Skin and dress the fish, but leave whole. Season inside and out with salt and pepper to taste. Brush inside and out with wine. Place the remainder of the wine in the bottom of a baking dish. Place the fish in the dish, but not touching. Sprinkle with paprika.

Cover and bake in a pre-heated 300° oven for 45 minutes or until tender. Uncover the last 15 minutes. Garnish with lemon slices.

CHAPTER XI

EELPOUT

*Eric Peterson, Gull Lake, Brainerd, Mn. with the
"ugly one" that tastes so good.*

Perhaps the ugliest freshwater fish that swims, but one of the most tasty, the eelpout is thrown back by most fishermen. How sad! After all, it is a freshwater codfish — a favorite saltwater variety. Known by several other names across North America — burbot, ling, or lawyer — it is preferred by many to any other fish.

Fried Fillets

2 pounds skinned fillets. Serves 4.
1 cup cracker crumbs
1 egg
1 cup water
1 T thyme
1 T oregano
1 T salt
1 T pepper
cooking oil, butter or margarine

Cut the fillets into serving size pieces. Combine the spices and sprinkle them over the cuts, about 1 t per side. Combine the egg and the water in a bowl. Place the cracker crumbs in a bowl. Dip the seasoned fillets in the egg wash and then in the cracker crumbs. Fry in a heavy skillet in a generous amount of oil over medium-high heat.

Fish Cakes

1 pound ground eelpout
3 cups mashed potatoes
¼ pound butter, softened
¼ cup light cream
1 t white pepper or freshly ground black pepper
1 T salt
cooking oil, butter or margarine

Combine all the ingredients and mold into patties.

Fry in oil over medium-high heat, turning once, so that both sides are a golden brown.

New England Chowder

2 pounds skinned fillets, cut into chunks
3 onions, sliced and broken into rings
4 large potatoes, peeled and cut into bite-size pieces
3 cups water
5 T salt
10 peppercorns
2 carrots, chunked
1 quart milk
1 cup cream

Bring the water to boiling. Add all ingredients except the fish, milk and cream. Bring to a boil and continue boiling until the potatoes and carrots are done. Stir in the milk and cream, add fish, bring to a boil, reduce heat and let simmer, covered, 20 minutes.

Mock Scallops

Because eelpout is a very firm meat and because it has a very mild flavor, the fillets may be cut up into the shapes of scallops — and few people will be able to tell the difference!

Cut the eelpout fillets into bite-size pieces — about the size of scallops.

Season with salt and pepper.
Dip in water-egg batter (1 egg to a cup of water).
Roll in cracker crumbs.

Fry in about ¼ inch oil, turning until brown on all sides. The crisper the better — but not burned. Serve hot.

Poached

Chunks of fillets are excellent poached (see recipes for poaching solutions on pages 82, 87 & 88) and then dipped into melted butter.

CHAPTER XII

WHITEFISH

The author with an 8½ pound whitefish, taken on a jig on the Lake of the Woods.

Whitefish are hard to come by for most anglers. In summer months they inhabit very deep water; they are usually found with lake trout. In those states where spearing through the ice is allowed, they are a fast-moving, sporty challenge. In some areas they may be netted in the fall of the year. Of course, they may be purchased in most fish markets. They make excellent eating, so give them a try.

Poached Whitefish

2 pounds of whitefish, scaled, cleaned and
  cut into chunks
1 onion, sliced
1 stalk dill (broken)
2 stalks celery, chopped
2 T salt
enough water to easily cover the fish pieces
  plus 2 cups

Place the onion, dill and celery in the water and bring to a boil. Reduce heat and let simmer 30 minutes. Remove 1½ cups of the liquid. Again bring to a boil and place the fish in the liquid. Let boil until fish flakes easily—usually about 15-20 minutes. Meanwhile, prepare a sauce from the following:

1½ cups of the fish stock you removed
1 T butter
1 T flour
1 t dill seed
1 egg, hard-boiled and chopped

Add all ingredients except the egg to the liquid. Let simmer 5 or 6 minutes. Add the chopped egg. Add salt and pepper if needed for your taste. Serve the fish with the sauce, over potatoes or pasta.

Instead of making a sauce, the pieces of fish may be dipped in melted butter and eaten like lobster.

Whitefish Roe *

Milk the roe from freshly netted whitefish into a clean container.

Rinse in a sieve.

Place in a bowl.

Finely chop one onion for each quart of roe. Gently stir in the onion and add salt and pepper to taste.

Let stand 24 hours under refrigeration.

Serve raw on crackers—a remarkable hors d'oeuvres.

Fish Eggs with Hen Eggs

Use sunfish, crappie, perch or whitefish roe and milt. The size of the roe sacks will vary with the type and size of the fish. Use about ½ cup of eggs and then add a pair of milt from the male fish for each pair of roe in the cup.

Sauté ¼ cup chopped onion in ¼ pound butter. You may wish to add a little garlic or other favorite spice. Add the eggs and milt, breaking their sacks and stir them together for a few minutes (using low heat). Meanwhile, beat two chicken eggs. Add to the fish eggs and milt, stirring them together. For added flavor, use a drop or two of Tabasco sauce or a teaspoon of soy sauce. Scramble and fry until done.

Serve with bacon and toast.

Milt Dishes

Milt, the sperm of the male fish, is a delicacy—particularly from whitefish, salmon, or members of the trout family. Remove the milt when you clean the fish; rinse it well in cold water, and remove the blue vein present with most fish. It is fragile and, therefore, should be handled with care. You may prepare milt with fish, using the same covering (flour or cracker crumbs, for example) or batter. As an hors d'oeuvres it is a delightful conversation piece. You will find it has a mild, rather sweet, non-fishy taste.

Milt also may be baked. Dip it first in milk or water and egg batter and then gently roll in crumbs or flour. Bake in a greased pan or baking dish.

It may even be used in casserole dishes as a fish substitute. Use alternate layers of milt, cracker or breadcrumbs, and mixed vegetables. Cover the whole thing with cream of mushroom soup.

Serve fried or baked milt with lemon or your favorite tartar sauce.

Baked Whitefish

Dress a large fish (at least 3 pounds live weight). Remove head, entrails, fins and scales.

Use any of the baking methods or stuffings given for muskies, northerns, salmon or lake trout.

Broiled with Bacon

2 pounds skinned fillets. Serves 4.

8 slices fat bacon

salt and pepper to taste

Season the fillets on both sides. Lightly coat a baking sheet with oil — or use foil. Place half the bacon under the fillets and half on top. Broil, turning once, until fish easily flakes with a fork at the larger end. Do not over-cook; it will be too dry. The bacon will add flavor and help keep the fillets from drying out.

*courtesy Joe Skala, Ely, Minnesota

CHAPTER XIII

SMELT

These little silvery fish from the Great Lakes—that drive normally sane people apparently out of their minds as they drive hundreds of miles and stay up half the night—are worth the effort, providing you eat them fresh. They are an oily fish and the flavor deteriorates rapidly. Keep them on (and in) crushed ice until you get home; then enjoy them immediately. They may be frozen in water and will still be good to eat, but not as delicious as fresh.

Smelt in Beer Batter
Smelt may be fried in flour or cracker crumbs, but are probably at their best deep fried in beer batter:

Pour one-half cup of beer into a bowl and let stand over-night or until "flat".

Add the beer and a tablespoon of cooking oil to two cups of white flour. Mix. Beat the whites of three eggs until stiff and work them into the batter. If mixture is too heavy, add a little water.

Dip the dressed smelt into the batter and deep fry in hot cooking oil (about 375°) until golden brown. The batter tends to insulate the fish so make certain they are done before serving.

Smelt in Barbecue Sauce

                    1 pound fresh smelt
      Ingredients:
                    1 - 8 ounce can tomato sauce
                    ½ cup chopped onion
                    2 T brown sugar
                    2 T vinegar
                    1 T Worcestershire sauce
                    1 T water
                    2 t prepared mustard
                    ¼ t salt

Clean, rinse and wipe smelt dry. Combine all ingredients, except smelt. Marinate smelt in tomato mixture, cover and refrigerate for several hours. In a large skillet bring smelt and tomato mixture to boiling. Reduce heat and simmer uncovered till fish are done. 8 to 10 minutes. Makes 3 to 4 servings.

CHAPTER XIV

FISH STOCK TARTAR SAUCES, HERBS AND SPICES

FISH STOCKS

Poaching Liquids

'Most any fish may be poached. First cut the fish into serving-size pieces. Plain water or water seasoned with salt may be used. The recipes which follow, however, will add special flavors to the fish. Do not over-cook. The time required will vary with the species of fish. Once the water has come to a rolling boil, as little as three minutes is required for some saltwater fish and as much as fifteen to twenty minutes for lake trout or pike.

After poaching fish, the liquid may be strained and frozen and used later for recipes calling for fish stalks.

Recipe #1 (a French recipe)
   Ingredients:
- 3 quarts of water
- 1 large onion, sliced
- 3 stalks celery, chopped
- 2 large carrots, sliced
- 2 bay leaves
- 2 T salt
- 6 peppercorns
- 4 T lemon juice
- 1 T minced herbs of your choosing (such as thyme, dill, tarragon, etc.)
- white wine (optional).

If wine is used, reduce the water by the number of cups added. No more than half the liquid need be wine.

Combine all ingredients in a cooking pot. Bring to a boil. Reduce the heat and let simmer—partially covered—for a full hour after the liquid starts to boil. Strain out and discard all solids. The liquid may be frozen for future use.

Recipe #2 (featuring cucumbers)
   Ingredients:
- 2 quarts water
- 2 cups white wine
- 1 large cucumber, sliced
- 1 stalk of dill, broken
- 2 bay leaves
- 12 peppercorns
- 2 T salt

Combine all ingredients in a cooking pot. Bring to a boil. Reduce heat and let simmer—partially covered—for an hour after it begins to boil. Fish may be added at this time or the solids may be strained out and just the liquid used for poaching. Liquid may be frozen for future use, but strain out the solids first.

Court Bouillon
  Ingredients:
                3 quarts water
                1 T butter
                1 t salt
                2 T lemon juice and the sliced rind
                3 peppercorns
                1 bay leaf
                ¼ cup sliced onion
                1 stalk celery, chopped
                1 carrot, sliced

Combine all ingredients. Bring to a boil, reduce heat and simmer for about 30 minutes. Sauce may be strained before using for poaching. The strained liquid may be frozen for future use.

Fish Stock #1
  Prepare fish stock for use in other recipes.

  Ingredients:
                fish trimmings, bones, head meat (or the whole head) 2 to 3 pounds
                2 large onions, sliced
                3 stalks celery
                3 bay leaves
                12 peppercorns
                1 T minced dill and/or other spices such as tarragon or thyme
                water
                white wine (optional)

Clean all fish parts. If you use heads, crack them with a hammer. If you choose not to use whole heads, cut out the cheeks and use them.

Place all ingredients in a cooking pot. Cover with water. (If you use wine, cover with equal parts of water and white wine.) Bring to a boil and then reduce heat; let simmer for about 1½ hours. Skin off any foam or solids that come to the surface as they form. Strain through very fine mesh screen or cloth. Keep the liquid and throw away the solids. The liquid may be frozen for future use.

Fish Stock #2

Ingredients:

2 pounds fish parts (heads, bones, trimmings)
$\frac{1}{4}$ pound butter
1 onion, large, sliced and separated into rings
4 T minced garlic
12 peppercorns
2 T thyme, chopped (dried)
1 t tarragon
6 cups red wine

Sauté the onion and fish until the onion is clear (about 3-4 minutes). Add $\frac{1}{3}$ of the wine. Continue cooking until the meat falls off the fish bones. The wine will be nearly evaporated. Add the rest of the wine and reduce heat so that the liquid will simmer but not boil, for about 1 hour. Strain out and discard all solids. Liquid may be frozen for future use.

TARTAR SAUCES

Caper Sauce
Ingredients:

>3 t capers
>3 small dill pickles
>3 t lemon juice
>dash of salt and pepper
>1 cup mayonnaise

Using a blender, combine the capers, pickles, lemon juice and seasonings. Using a spoon, stir the mixture into the mayonnaise. Refrigerate.

Pickle Relish Sauce
Ingredients:

>1 cup mayonnaise
>3 T sweet pickle relish
>1 t minced onion
>½ t tarragon

Blend together all ingredients. Refrigerate.

Garlic Sauce
Ingredients:

>2 T minced garlic
>2 eggs (yolks only)
>2 T lemon juice
>1 cup olive oil
>1 t mustard
>salt and pepper to taste

Using a blender or food processor, briefly blend all ingredients except the olive oil. Then, slowly add the olive oil and blend until the mixture has a mayonnaise-like consistency. Refrigerate.

Red Sauce #1
    Ingredients:
           1 - 12 oz. bottle chili sauce
           3 T horseradish
           3 T lemon juice
    Blend all ingredients. Refrigerate.

Red Sauce #2
           $\frac{1}{2}$ cup chili sauce
           $\frac{1}{3}$ cup catsup
           $\frac{1}{3}$ cup horseradish
           $1\frac{1}{2}$ t Worcestershire sauce
           2 T lemon juice
           $\frac{1}{8}$ t pepper
           $\frac{1}{4}$ cup minced celery or 1 T celery seeds
    Refrigerate.

Sour Cream Sauce
           $\frac{1}{2}$ cup mayonnaise
           $\frac{1}{2}$ cup sour cream
           2 T minced onion or chives or green onions
           2 T mustard
           2 T chopped dill
           dash salt and pepper
    Combine the mustard, sour cream and mayonnaise. Then blend in the onion, dill and seasonings. Refrigerate.

Cucumber-Dill Sauce
           1 cup sour cream
           1 medium cucumber (peeled, seeded and chopped fine)
           1 T minced dill
           3 T mayonnaise
           1 T lemon juice
           salt and pepper to taste
    Blend all ingredients. Refrigerate.

SEASONINGS FOR FISH

In addition to the old standbys of salt and pepper, try some of the following:

Lemon Herbs*
Lightly season with salt and pepper, then sprinkle on lemon-herb mixture.

Lemon Pepper*
Substitute for regular black pepper.

White Pepper*
Substitute white pepper for black pepper, particularly with white-meated fish (for sake of appearance).

Marinades
Using 'most any of the sauce recipes on the previous pages, marinate the fillets before frying (refrigerate) for about 30 minutes to 1 hour.

Seasoned Oil or Butter
Season melted butter with favorite herbs or spices. Fry the fish in this seasoned butter or oil.

Seasoned Sautéing
As the fish is sautéed, sprinkle minced or chopped herbs over the fish—such as tarragon, garlic, dill, paprika, thyme, parsley or coriander (or combinations thereof). Or these seasonings may be added just before serving.

Seasoned Cracker Crumbs or Other Breading
When frying fish coated with cracker crumbs, flour or other dry ingredients, add any (or a mixture) of the dry seasonings listed above to the crumbs; stir thoroughly.

Seasoned Batter (for deep frying in oil)
Stir in any of the seasonings listed above.

*available in most supermarkets.

SUGGESTIONS FOR USING SPECIFIC HERBS AND SPICES

Capers, which are really unopened flower buds from the caper plant, are an excellent addition to almost any sauce.

Marjoram is a powerful herb and should be used sparingly.

Dill weed or seeds may be used; the flavor is stronger in the seeds.

Rosemary is another strong herb and should be used with caution.

Sage is traditionally used with poultry, but is appropriate for fish stuffing.

Tarragon is a universal seasoning but tends to be bitter if used in excess.

Thyme tends to be overpowering and should be used with caution.

Oregano is sharp and spicy.

Basil is especially good with dishes using tomatoes.

Bay Leaf is one of the stronger seasonings and one or two leaves is usually enough for stews, soups, fish stock, etc.

As a rule of thumb, dried herbs and spices are nearly twice as potent as equal volume of fresh.

NOTES

Other Books by Duane R. Lund

A Beginner's Guide to Hunting and Trapping
A Kid's Guidebook to Fishing Secrets
Fishing and Hunting Stories from The Lake of the Woods
Andrew, Youngest Lumberjack
The Youngest Voyageur
White Indian Boy
Gull Lake, Yesterday and Today
Lake of the Woods, Yesterday and Today, Vol. 1
Lake of the Woods, Earliest Accounts, Vol. 2
Lake of the Woods (The Last 50 Years and the Next)
Leech Lake, Yesterday and Today
The North Shore of Lake Superior, Yesterday and Today
Our Historic Boundary Waters
Our Historic Upper Mississippi
Tales of Four Lakes and a River
The Indian Wars
Chief Flatmouth
101 Favorite Freshwater Fish Recipes
101 Favorite Wild Rice Recipes
101 Favorite Mushroom Recipes
150 Ways to Enjoy Potatoes
Early Native American Recipes and Remedies
Camp Cooking, Made Easy and Fun
Cooking Minnesotan, yoo-betcha!
more than 50 Ways to enjoy Lefse
Entertainment Helpers, Quick and Easy
Nature's Bounty for Your Table
Sauces, Seasonings and Marinades for Fish and Wild Game
The Scandinavian Cookbook
The Soup Cookbook
Traditional Holiday Ethnic Recipes - collected all over the world
The Life And Times of THREE POWERFUL OJIBWA CHIEFS,
Curly Head Hole-In-The-Day the elder, Hole-In-The-Day the younger
Hasty But Tasty
Fruit and Nut Recipes
Europeans In North America *Before Columbus*
Hunting and Fishing in Alaska
German Home Cooking
Italian Home Cooking
Eating Green and Loving It

About the Author

- EDUCATOR (Retired, Superintendent of Schools, Staples, Minnesota);
- HISTORIAN (Past Member of Executive Board, Minnesota Historical Society);
  Past Member of BWCA and National Wilderness Trails Advisory Committees;
- SENIOR CONSULTANT to the Blandin Foundation
- WILDLIFE ARTIST, OUTDOORSMAN.